The Readers House

ISSUE 37
May 01, 2023
thereadershouse.co.uk
GLOBAL EDITION

INTER
GO
Azure
SUS
Au
of

INTERVIEW
with Acclaimed
Authors
KAYIL YORK
ROSE ROBINS
DANA BURTIN
MEDUSA STONE
VANESSA GROSSETT
MCCOLLONOUGH CEILI
RUSS WILLIAMS

Makes Every Book Extra Special
NEIL PERRY GORDON ☆INTERVIEW

JANE GREEN
New York Times
Bestselling Author

She is the greatest
CAROLYN BONE

Aut Vincam, Aut Periam;
I will either conquer or Perish!
C.H. ADMIRAND

available at

amazon

Dive

Into a
Great
Journey

Ready to
share
your
story?

The Reader's House
Make a phenomenal start
thereadershouse.co.uk

A good book
will keep you
fascinated
for days.
A good bookshop
for your
whole life.

Waterstones

IN THIS ISSUE

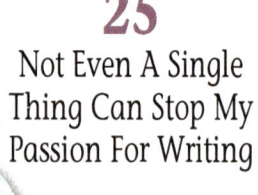

EDITOR'S LETTER

We are thrilled to bring you this issue of The Reader's House, featuring exclusive interviews with some of the most acclaimed authors of our time. Our pages are filled with insights and inspiration from a diverse group of writers, each with their own unique voice and perspective.

On the cover of this issue featuring an exclusive interview with Neil Perry Gordon, an acclaimed novelist who has found success by combining historical fiction with the metaphysical.

In our interview, Mr. Gordon shares his unique approach to storytelling, which he describes as "an exploration of the human condition through the lens of history and spirituality." He explains how he weaves together historical events and figures with mystical elements to create a compelling narrative that captivates readers and inspires them to think deeply about the world around them.

We also delve into Mr. Gordon's writing process, his inspirations, and his upcoming projects. As you will discover, he is a writer with a deep passion for storytelling and a profound understanding of the power of literature to connect us to our past and our future.

In our interviews with Kayil York, Rose Robins, Dana Burtin, Medusa Stone, Vanessa Grossett, McCollonough Ceili, and Russ Williams, we explore the creative process, the challenges and joys of writing, and the many ways that literature can transform our lives. From Kayil York's poignant reflections on the power of storytelling to Rose RobIns' insights on the importance of representation in literature, these interviews offer a wealth of knowledge and inspiration for writers and readers alike.

Whether you are an aspiring writer looking for guidance and inspiration, or a reader seeking new voices and fresh perspectives, this issue of The Reader's House has something for you. We invite you to immerse yourself in the world of literature and explore the stories that make us human. So sit back, relax, and immerse yourself in the world of Neil Perry Gordon, and other acclaimed authors.

Enjoy reading

PUBLISHER
The Reader's House
A Subsidiary of Newyox Media

200 Suite
134-146 Curtain Road
EC2A 3AR London
t: +44 79 3847 8420

editor@thereadershouse.co.uk
thereadershouse.com

EDITORIAL
A. Harlowe
editor@thereadershouse.co.uk
Dan Peters
dan.peters@thereadershouse.co.uk
Ben Alan
ben.alan@thereadershouse.co.uk

COVER ILLUSTRATION
Dila Tanrikulu C.
/dilatanrikuluc

CONTRIBUTOS
Claudine D. Reyes
Andrea Piacquadio
Adrian T. Cheng
Donna Schim
Jon Allo
Tim Halloran
Mickey Mikkelson
Oleg Magni
Amir SeilSepour
Bill Youngblood
Jetty Stutzman
Jimmy Choo
Peter Filinovich
Rrodnae Productions

The Reader's House
thereadershouse.co.uk

Novelist Finds Success Joining Genres — Historical Fiction with the Metaphysical

NEIL PERRY GORDON

An Exclusive Conversation

BY BEN F. ONCU

Neil Perry Gordon, Beginning with his debut novel — A Cobbler's Tale, followed by Moon Flower, The

"I'm going through a giant obsession with Neil Gordon. His writing style is absolutely captivating, and his stories are so much fun. With conventions and book signings starting back up, I have been doing lots of driving and listening to audiobooks while on the road. I'm hooked on all the books Neil narrates. I just want to listen to him tell me stories.

Righteous One, The Bomb Squad, Hope City, Sadie's Sin, Cape Nome, Otzi's Odyssey, Denali,

Thunder Falls, and most recently — The Nazarite, Neil Perry Gordon has established himself as a well-respected, prolific novelist of historical and metaphysical fiction. His storytelling abilities has earned him high editorial praise from the likes of Kirkus, Midwest Book Review, Book Viral and others, including hundreds of four and five star reader reviews on Amazon and Goodreads.

Neil attributes his

love of the writing process to his formative education at the Green Meadow Waldorf School, where he understood that classes such as music, dance and theater, writing, literature, legends and myths, were not simply subjects to be learned, but instead lessons to be experienced.

His creative writing methods and inspiration have been described as organic; meaning he begins his work with a premise for his characters, rather than working within the confines of a formal, detailed outline. This encourages his writing to offer surprising twists and unexpected outcomes, which readers have celebrated. His novels have the attributes of being driven by an equal balance between character development and face-paced action, which moves his stories along at a swift page-turning pace.

Can you share with our readers how you grew up?

I was raised among the wilds of a distant suburb, where I built forts in the woods, swam with bullfrogs in muddy ponds, and regardless of the weather, played ball until my mother called me in for dinner. My

Continued *on page 10*

"I have published ten novels and a novella in the past five years. To produce this amount of work, I must write every day. This discipline or dare I say—obsession, has allowed me to take great strides in the quality of my storytelling. Of course, if I hadn't had good reviews, I wouldn't have persevered. It is truly satisfying to hear from readers about my books."

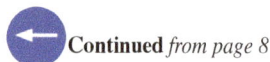

Continued *from page 8*

school days were where I learned that music, art, theater, writing, legends, and myths were not courses simply to be studied, memorized, and tested, but instead lessons to be lived and experienced. Meanwhile, during my youth, Father taught me the intricacies of owning and managing a retail business. One that supported our family along with serving the needs of a community.

"In one word—perseverance. I have published ten novels and a novella in the past five years. To produce this amount of work, I must write every day. This discipline or dare I say— obsession, has allowed me to take great strides in the quality of my storytelling."

Was there a single book that inspired you to become a writer?

The one book I attribute as the source driving my writer's inspiration is Shantaram. It is hard to find another author with the same ability to transform prose into poetry like David Gregory Roberts. When in need, I reach for one of his memorable passages and relish in the marvelous ways he weaves our most sensitive emotions into his storytelling.

Was there an event in your life that has inspired your writing?

On January 27th, 2021, my thirty-two-year-old son passed away. This tragic moment had a massive effect upon me, which in turn began my quest of trying to understand the journey of my son's soul. I wanted to learn how to pierce the veil between our two worlds in order to maintain our connection. What I've learned is that my fiction writing is not only a wonderful way of delving into the metaphysical world, but is also a spiritual practice. This examination blossomed into an idea that our biography is not limited to our time on earth, but continues on into our soul life, creating an infinite loop of an eternal story.

What habits have contributed the most to you becoming a successful writer?

In one word—per-

severance. I have published ten novels and a novella in the past five years. To produce this amount of work, I must write every day. This discipline or dare I say—obsession, has allowed me to take great strides in the quality of my storytelling. Of course, if I hadn't had good reviews, I wouldn't have persevered. It is truly satisfying to hear from readers about my books.

How would you describe your writing process?

My writing process can be described as organic, meaning I begin with a premise for my characters and let the story unfold from there, rather than working from a detailed outline. This approach results in surprising twists and unexpected outcomes, which readers have celebrated. My novels are known for its balance betft pace.

What are the greatest challenges you face as an author?

The greatest challenge in my writing

"What I've learned is that my fiction writing is not only a wonderful way of delving into the metaphysical world, but is also a spiritual practice."

career has been creating awareness of my work. There are so many books being written and offered, which is great as a reader, but difficult for the author to gain notoriety. Hopefully, with publications such as The Reader's House, I can reach a wider audience.

What's the last great book you read?

The Midnight Library by Matt Haig

DENALI

The Alaskan Adventures of Percy Hope – The Goldfield Trilogy – Book 3 (June 2022)

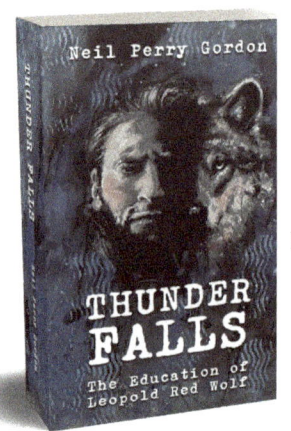

THUNDER FALLS

The Education of Leopold Red Wolf – (February 2023)

NEIL PERRY GORDON

CAPE NOME

Neil Perry Gordon

NOVELIST

On January 27th, 2021, my thirty-two-year-old son passed away. This tragic moment had a massive effect upon me, which in turn began my quest of trying to understand the journey of my son's soul. I wanted to learn how to pierce the veil between our two worlds in order to maintain our connection.

You're organizing a party. Which two authors, dead or alive, do you invite?

Isaac Asimov and Ray Bradbury

What do you read when you're working on a book?

I seek out inspiring, poetic prose, even though my writing is not embellished in a similar way.

And what kind of reading do you avoid while writing?

I avoid complex plot novels, as I want to keep my creative process un-incumbered by another writer's storytelling strategies.

What moves you most in a work of literature?

Evocative, meaning-ful and generational sweeping tales. Such epics fuels my creativity and encourages me to improve the quality of my novels.

What genres do you especially enjoy reading?

I'm an avid reader of Historical Fiction and a writer of the same. I also enjoy tales infused with a healthy dose of the metaphysical.

What book are you planning to read next?

The Creative Act – A Way of Being by Rick Rubin

What books and authors have impacted your writing career?

Stein on Writing by Sol Stein. Steven King on Writing by Steven King. Story by Robert McKee.

Which writer would you want to write your life story?

If he were still alive, I would select Ray Bradbury.

What books do you find yourself returning to again and again?

Tales of Alhambra by Washington Irving. The Foundation Series by Isaac Asimov.

What books are you embarrassed not to have read yet?

Infinite Jest by David Foster Wallace. The Name of the Rose by Umberto Eco ●

Continued *on page 12*

**Continued** *from page 11*

STORIES BY NEIL PERRY GORDON

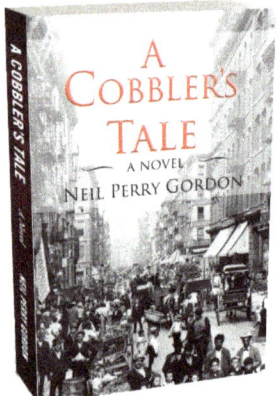

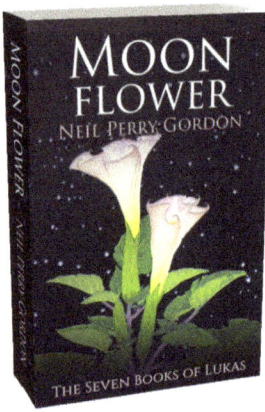

A COBBLER'S TALE

Jewish Immigrants Story of Survival, from Eastern Europe to New York's Lower East Side – Book 1 (October 2018)

MOON FLOWER

A Seventeenth Century Tale of a Young Man's Search for the Great Spirit (February 2019)

THE RIGHTEOUS ONE

A Cobbler's Journey into the Dreamworld and Beyond – Book 2 (September 2019)

THE BOMB SQUAD

Clash of the Patriots (April 2020)

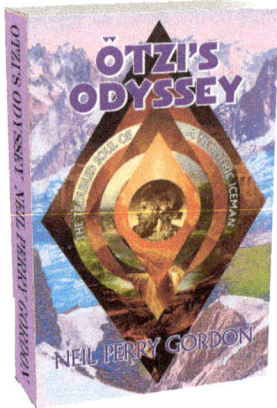

HOPE CITY

The Alaskan Adventures of Percy Hope – The Goldfield Trilogy – Book 1 (May 2020)

SADIE'S SIN

The Zwi Migdal's Reign of Terror (November 2020)

CAPE NOME

The Alaskan Adventures of Percy Hope – The Goldfield Trilogy – Book 2 (March 2021)

OTZI'S ODYSSEY

The Troubled Soul of a Neo-lithic Iceman (January 2022)

🌐 neilperrygordon.com

NeilPerryGordon

NeilPerryGordon

WELCOME HOME – UNEXPECTEDLY USEFUL HOUSEWARMING GIFTS

Flowers are always a great way to brighten a day, but why not offer something that can brighten a space for years to come and grow with the household? Bring over a gorgeous houseplant or orchid for a gift that lasts and makes your friends think of you every time they see it. Tie on a sweet note and a ribbon for a fun, personal touch.

PHOTO BY STATEPOINT

Attending a housewarming is a great way to celebrate a friend's new home, but how do you find the perfect present to accompany the visit? These unique gift ideas are not only bound to make a statement, they're incredibly useful to boot.

Fix-It Essentials: For practicality at its absolute best, pack up some must-haves for the house. Include a hammer, screwdrivers and some Original Duck Tape brand duct tape to help your friends get all those initial DIY projects handled – and cover bases for any future projects and everyday fixes that may pop up.

Plant Some Love: Flowers are always a great way to brighten a day, but why not offer something that can brighten a space for years to come and grow with the household? Bring over a gorgeous houseplant or orchid for a gift that lasts and makes your friends think of you every time they see it. Tie on a sweet note and a ribbon for a fun, personal touch.

Organization Must-Haves: Create a welcome home gift that will prove useful for years to come. Put together a basket that includes all those essentials we sometimes forget, like high-quality hangers, drawer organizers, rubber bands and paper clips for paperwork. Include additional essentials, such as Duck Max Strength Nano-Grab Gel Tape for securing miscellaneous items, photos and temporary seasonal décor, along with EasyLiner Brand Shelf Liner with Clorox for upgraded home organization.

Stock the Bar: Wine is fine, but why not equip your friends with what they need to entertain in the future? Bring over a favorite spirit, mixer and cocktail recipe book to keep the party going. Round out this gift with a cute set of rocks glasses or drink shaker.

Take a Photo: In the age of digital photography, you can help make memories more permanent. Bring your newly relocated friends a large empty photo album and toss in a few disposable cameras or instant film camera to start capturing the fun right away. Kick off the entries by including a cute photo of yourself!

Gift giving at a housewarming doesn't have to be stressful. By getting creative with a variety of useful items, you can help make a house a home while making a lasting impression on those you love.

New prepared pot pie, strength plates of mixed greens, wood-let go pizzas, pasta, sandwiches, burgers, and more.'Company Name's heated merchandise and treats, including our Six-Layer Chocolate Motherlode Cake, Scratch Carrot Cake, and delectably rich cream cheddar pies are prevalent top choices with our visitors. (StatePoint)

"Gift giving at a housewarming doesn't have to be stressful. By getting creative with a variety of useful items, you can help make a house a home while making a lasting impression on those you love."

BOOKS, SATISFIES THE NEED

A conversation with
KAYIL YORK

Author of Brave Soul

" Red wine is her lifeblood and gin and tonic is a joy. For as long as she can remember she has been using writing as an outlet for all of life's circumstances.

Kayil York is a writer from Houston, TX. She is a Mother, Wife, and passionate writes. Red wine is her lifeblood and gin and tonic is a joy. For as long as she can remember she has been using writing as an outlet for all of life's circumstances. It has been a way to help others with their lives, as well as a means of showing them that their ends are only new beginnings. She writes in hopes to inspire others to stand strong and to not give up on themselves no matter how hard life hits.

What's the last great book you read?

Good Boundaries and Goodbyes by Lysa Terkeurst

What's your favorite book no one else has heard of?

Rooms by James Rubart

You're organizing a party. Which two authors, dead or alive, do you invite?

Edgar Allan Poe and Jane Austin

Who are your favorite writers? Are there any who aren't as widely known as they should be, whom you'd recommend in particular?

Stephanie Bennett, Madalina Coman, Ruby Dahl, Topher Kearby, Matt Spencer, Kalen Dion, Madalyn Beck, Morgan Olivier.

What do you read when you're working on a book? And what kind of reading do you avoid while writing?

Self help/growth books that challenge me or brings out the things I've learned about over the years so I can put those lessons to paper. I mainly listen to music- that's more of a muse to me when writing.

What moves you most in a work of literature?

The way the writer uses words, if it doesn't move me within the first few pages it's hard to continue reading.

What genres do you especially enjoy reading?

Self help/person growth, poetry, romance, mystery/thrillers

Who is your favorite fictional hero or heroine?

Angel from Redeeming Love - her resiliency was entirely moving and inspiring.

What kind of reader were you as a child?

I loved any and all books

Have you ever changed your opinion of a book based on information about the author, or anything else?

I Have never changed my opinion. I have merely been fascinated more to know how the author came to write what they did. To know how they delved into their mind to write such a work.

Which writer would you want to write your life story?

Lysa Terkeurst

What books do you find yourself returning to again and again?

Redeeming Love

What do you plan to read next?

12 Rules for Life by Jordan Peterson

Aut Vincam, Aut Periam:
I'll either Conquer or Perish!

C.H. ADMIRAND

C.H. Admirand was born in Aiken, South Carolina, but her parents moved back to northern New Jersey where she grew up.

She believes in fate, destiny, and love at first sight. C.H. fell in love at first sight when she was seventeen. She was married for 41 wonderful years until her husband lost his battle with cancer. Soul mates, their hearts will be joined forever.

They have three grown children—one son-in-law, two grandsons, two rescue dogs, and two rescue grand-cats.

Her characters rarely follow the synopsis she outlines for them...but C.H. has learned to listen to her characters! Her heroes always have a few of her husband's best qualities: his honesty, his integrity, his compassion for those in need, and his killer broad shoulders. C.H. writes about the things she loves most: Family, her Irish and English Ancestry, Baking and Gardening.

"C.H. Admirand's Purcell ancestors' family motto, and her promise to her husband when he was losing his battle with Pancreatic Cancer to keep writing, gave her the strength to continue writing after losing the love of her life and keeper of her heart."

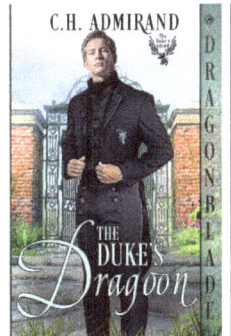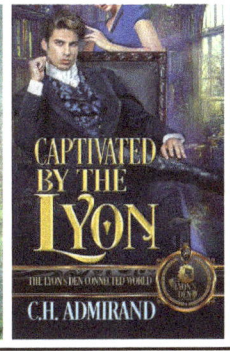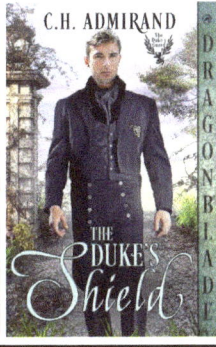

C.H. Admirand received Dragonblade Publishing's Bestselling Author Award for September 2002 for The Duke's Sword (The Duke's Guard, Book One.)

Who are your favorite writers?

Nora Roberts, Julie Garwood, and Kit Morgan—all of whom I re-read. I discovered Nora Roberts attending my first NJRW Writer's Conference in 1995 and became an instant fan of her Contemporary Romances. My neighbor introduced me to Julie Garwood's Medieval and Regency Historicals. I discovered Kit Morgan when my husband was in the hospital, and I wasn't sleeping nights—thank God for my e-reader! She swept me away with her Sweet Prairie Romances.

What genres do you especially enjoy reading?

Historical and Contemporary Romance—and their sub-genres: Small Town Romance, Romantic Suspense, Regency-era Historicals, Medieval Romance, Time Travel Romance, and Western Historical Romance.

What do you read when you are working on a book? And what kind of reading do you avoid while writing?

I'm currently writing my fourteenth Regency Historical Romance for Dragonblade Publishing. After spending so much time immersed in 1815 England, I need to read something completely different! I just finished reading Lynn Shannon's, Tactical Force: Christian Romantic Suspense (Triumph Over Adversity Book 6)

What kind of a reader were you as a child?

A voracious—under the covers with a flashlight after "lights out"—kind of reader.

What is the single most important advice you give to aspiring authors?

NEVER give up and remember rejections are not personal—publishing is a business. You never know just how close you are to achieving your goal of becoming a published author if you give up. I was rejected 99 times with a number of different books before I received "the call" in 2000. My first book was published in 2001.

Have you ever received an invitation to write for a publisher?

In 2019, I received an invitation to submit a Regency Historical series to Dragonblade Publishing. I had been writing contemporary romance for a number of years, but decided to accept the challenge and stretch my writing muscles. My proposal was accepted. I signed my first contract with them, and three months later I met the first of four deadlines. But life isn't for the faint of heart, and two months later my husband was diagnosed with Pancreatic Cancer.

How long have you been writing, and how many books have you published?

I have always loved to write poetry and short stories, but in 1994, I started writing with the goal of being published. In 1995, I joined Romance Writers of America (RWA) and NJRW (New Jersey Romance Writers) and began my journey, honing my craft, and learning the ins and outs of the publishing industry. I received the call in 2000 and my first novel, The Marshal's Destiny, was published in 2001. As of today, I have forty-one books published, with five more due before the end of the year.

If you could meet any writer, dead or alive, who would it be?

Jane Austen, Cicely Mary Barker, and Sir Arthur Conan Doyle. I'd love to sit down and chat about our writing processes over a cup of tea—I'd even bake the cream scones!

AdmirandH

CHAdmirandAuthor

chadmirand.com

SHE IS THE ARCHITECT OF DREAMS

"CAROLYN BOWEN is a mystery author who calls on her life escapades and an adventurous, imaginative spirit to inspire and entertain."

A conversation with

CAROLYN M. BOWEN

Author of 15 Titles

CAROLYN BOWEN is an award-winning mystery thriller author who calls on her life escapades and an adventurous, imaginative spirit to inspire and entertain. Bowen uses travel as a muse to explore cultures and dialogue to bring her stories to life. Her writing credits include Cross-Ties, The Long Road Home, The Sydney Jones Series, and The Legacy Series.

What's your favorite book no one else has heard of?

A fan gifted me White Orchid by Henrietta Mason. I'd never heard of Mason, but after reading the novel I felt honored to read her story. Since then, I have usually re-read it once a year. The mystery is exceptional, and the scenic descriptions are so real they feel touchable.

You're organizing a party. Which two authors, dead or alive, do you invite?

The two authors I'd invite for an interesting conversation

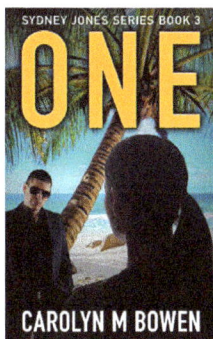

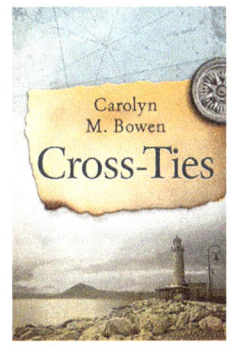
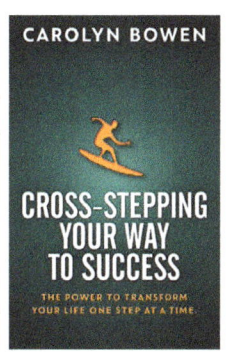
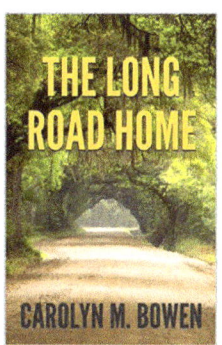

"Very great world building along with interesting character development. An overall great read that will keep you on the edge of your seat wanting more!"

- Jotherynn Halterman

would be Sidney Sheldon and Agatha Christie. They are both masters of the craft of writing and have unique backstories.

Which writers — working today do you admire most?

My all-time favorites of writers working today are John Grisham and David Baldacci. John Grisham is a literary legend and doesn't miss a beat delivering exacting legal-speak with a surreal plot that'll keep you flipping the pages to the end.

Baldacci is a master storyteller who brings his characters to life. The Good, bad,

> My all-time favorites of writers working today are John Grisham and David Baldacci.

and ugly come together in a twisty plot filled with murderous intent and surprising conclusions. I can't wait to read his latest release.

What do you read when you're working on a book? And what kind of reading do you avoid while writing?

When I'm writing I read books about the craft of writing and marketing books. I avoid reading novels in the genre I'm writing in to keep my thoughts focused on my story.

What moves you most in a work of literature?

My favorite works of literature have believable characters willing to express a broad range of emotions given the situation. I especially enjoy natural and scenic settings as a backdrop for the story to unfold.

What genres do you especially enjoy reading?

The genre I read most often is mystery-thrillers with an underlying romantic theme.

Who is your favorite fictional hero or heroine?

James Bond.

What books and authors have impacted your writing career?

From an early age, Around the World in Eighty Days by the French writer Jules Verne captured my attention and fueled my love for travel and adventure. Later, the books by author Sidney Sheldon inspired me to write my own stories. A

> As a child, I was a prolific reader and when bored would read The World Book Encyclopedia to learn new words and their meaning.

nod to him was incorporated in naming my Sydney Jones Series.

What kind of reader were you as a child?

As a child, I was a prolific reader and when bored would read The World Book Encyclopedia to learn new words and their meaning. The fondness for learning is a lifelong habit that makes life interesting.

Have you ever changed your opinion of a book based on information about the author, or anything else?

No, I've never changed my mind about an author or book I've read. Everyone has a right to their opinions and I respect their choices.

If you could meet any writer, dead or alive, who would it be? And what would you want to know?

My love of writing life was inspired by Ernest Hemingway and his real-life adventures. I'd love to talk to him about his living at his hilltop villa, Finca Vigia east of Havana for nearly two decades and his experiences off the coast aboard his 38-foot fishing boat, Pilar.

My fascination with his adventures in Cuba made their way into Chance: A Novel, book 2 in my Sydney Jones Series.

What do you plan to read next?

I'm working on the next novel in my Legacy Series and that means I'm steering clear of reading in my favorite genre. The latest book on my reading list is The Copywriter's Handbook by Robert W. Bly, and that'll keep me busy during breaks from writing.

🌐 cmbowenauthor.com

🐦 CMBowenAuthor

📘 CarolynBowenAuthor/

"My Risky Romance In Turkey" Brings Delight to Readers Young and Old

My Risky Romance In Turkey" Brings Delight to Readers Young and Old

When a woman breaks up with her boyfriend during a long trip thousands of miles away from home, you know something outrageous is about to happen.

A romance-adventure memoir, written by author Karen Carlson is about to stir emotions and enthall readers across the world through the book, "My Risky Romance in Turkey".

The book talks about a true story of Karen, the author, who started a long trip with her boyfriend, Cap. Unfortunately, Karen's feelings for him quickly ended as he became more interested in drugs than anything else in Europe. And that's where the exhilarating adventure story kicks off.

Cap returns home and Karen decides to stay overseas permanently. Soon, Karen became interested in a Turkish man, and started a romance with him. But odd situations started to come into play. Soon, people were warning Karen that she is in danger. Others told her there was no problem. Karen's adventure turns from romance to fear, questions, and ambiguity.

Will Karen ever find out what is happening, and who this Turkish man truly is? Will her life be put in harm's way? When will her fears end?

Nicki, an Amazon verified customer who describes the book "An Adventurous Memoir" writes a review: "This memoir has everything. Romance, adventure, and the interaction with the good and the bad." Since the book's release in June 2022, the book has garnered a handful of awesome reviews from its readers.

When asked how she wrote the book, Karen says that she originally wrote the book to give to her parents and sister as they have been very worried about her travels and whereabouts. "I gave them the manuscript as a gift - to show them the details of my trip to Turkey. Eventually it turned out to be a beautiful piece of literature that is meant to be shared to the world," Karen continues.

It is Karen's intention that the book will be read by passionate travelers who want to explore more about their lives through traveling. "I believe people can learn a lot from it - the differences in life in other countries. I hope readers will be reminded to pay attention to the different laws and behaviors - and to do their best to be safe whenever they go," she says.

Karen now works in Miami, Florida with her husband and two cats. She has traveled to and explored more than 100 countries. Her main interests in her travels are always the culture, the various foods she's introduced to, and then her studying and learning foreign languages.

"My Risky Romance In Turkey" is now available on Amazon and other leading digital bookstore platforms worldwide.

CLASSES

DEBUT NOVEL TAKES READER ON A QUEST TO FIND HOPE IN DESPAIR, COMFORT IN BETRAYAL AND HEALING IN PAIN

By Erik Olin Wright

The most impressive book on class I have read in some years'
MICHAEL MANN, author of
The Dark Side of Democracy

Class analysis and class struggle are central concepts in Marx's social theory yet, notoriously, Marx never wrote a systematic exposition of these terms during his lifetime, and succeeding generations have had to piece together interpretations from his many scattered references and discussions. The problem of trying to develop a Marxist class analysis on this basis has been made all the more acute by changes in the class structure of advanced capitalism, for these have thrown up a bewildering range of new social strata which seem to be difficult to reconcile with the many traditional understandings of class.

In Classes, Erik Olin Wright, one of the foremost Marxist sociologists and class theorists, rises to the twofold challenge of both clarifying the abstract, structural account of class implicit in Marx, and of applying and refining the account in the light of contemporary developments in advanced capitalist societies. Recentering the concept of class on the process of exploitation, Wright discusses his famous notion of "contradictory class locations" in relation to the empirical complexities of the middle class, and he provides an analysis of class structure in "post-capitalist" societies. Wright then goes on to draw out the implications of his approach and to submit it to detailed empirical testing with the use of a trans-national survey of class structure and consciousness.

PRAISE

"The most impressive book on class I have read in some years."—Michael Mann, Contemporary Sociology

"An empirically supported reformulation of class theory that achieves exemplary standards of critique, complexity and clarity."—Claus Offe

"Erik Olin Wright's Classes is almost certain to be the most important book on social classes this decade … The book presents a major breakthrough in the conceptualization of class relations … and it will be required reading for all macro-sociologists."—American Journal of Sociology

Hike

By Pete Oswald
Illustrated by
Pete Oswald

Take to the trails for a celebration of nature — and a day spent with dad.

In the cool and quiet early light of morning, a father and child wake up. Today they're going on a hike. Follow the duo into the mountains as they witness the magic of the wilderness, overcome challenges, and play a small role in the survival of the forest. By the time they return home, they feel alive — and closer than ever — as they document their hike and take their place in family history. In detail-rich panels and textured panoramas, Pete Oswald perfectly paces this nearly wordless adventure, allowing readers to pause for subtle wonders and marvel at the views. A touching tribute to the bond between father and child, with resonant themes for Earth Day, Hike is a breath of fresh air.

PRAISE

The beauty of the natural world is viewed through the lens of the relationship between parent and child; their closeness is what gives this outdoor experience meaning. On the way home, their eyes meet in the rear-view mirror; they know they've shared something special, a moment underscored by a final spread of the two cuddling on the sofa.
—Publishers Weekly (starred review)

The relationship between the father and child makes this not just a picture book set in the outdoors, but a warm expression of how memories are created and bonds form. Like the woods, this book is an immersive experience that invites repeated visits.
—Kirkus Reviews (starred review)

The handsome digital artwork clearly expresses the characters' emotions as well as the beauty and majesty of the natural world...A near-wordless book seems a particularly appropriate way of communicating the quiet yet powerful experience of walking through a wilderness area. A memorable picture book on enjoying the natural world.
—Booklist (starred review)

Painted landscapes conjure the soft haze of for-est waterfalls, mountain vistas, watery strokes of tree branches, small details of flowers, woodland creatures, and the warm expressions between parent and child. A suggested first purchase for all libraries, this visual feast evokes a breath-taking climb to the heights, where the absence of text reflects the serenity of the mountain and those who quietly rejoice in the hike.
—School Library Journal (starred review)

There's gentle humor throughout, and the loving relationship between this father and child enjoying the outdoors together is movingly emphasized. Oswald's use of earth tones and textures reinforces the beauty of the natural world and the importance of sustaining it through simple family traditions like this one.
—The Horn Book (starred review)

Oswald's Klassen-esque figures of the wide-eyed, dark-skinned dad and kid feature in the smaller panels but they're appropriately dwarfed by the majesty of the woods in larger spreads... the outing is a sunny celebration of the outdoors

and of sharing a strenuous but beautiful day of exploration. Many kids will long to follow suit, and maybe this will prompt some new family excursions.
—Bulletin of the Center for Children's Books

The lush digital artwork is full of details for careful observers. The use of white space and absence of any sort of panel lines gives the whole undertaking a clean quality, like breathing in fresh mountain air...A beautiful book about family, perseverance, and the Great Outdoors.
—Travis Jonker, 100 Scope Notes

ABOUT THE AUTHOR

MAGGIE SHIPSTEAD is the New York Times-bestselling author of three novels and a short story collection. Her novel Great Circle was shortlisted for the Booker Prize and is currently a finalist for the Women's Prize. She is a graduate of the Iowa Writers' Workshop, the recipient of a fellowship from the National Endowment for the Arts, and the winner of the Dylan Thomas Prize and the L.A. Times Book Prize for First Fiction. She lives in Los Angeles.

Maggie Shipstead is available for select speaking engagements. To inquire about a possible speaking appearance, please contact Penguin Random House Speakers Bureau at speakers@penguinrandomhouse.com or visit www.prh-speakers.com

ALSO BY MAGGIE SHIPSTEAD

GREAT CIRCLE

NEW YORK TIMES BESTSELLER • A TODAY SHOW #ReadWithJenna BOOK CLUB PICK • The unforgettable story of a daredevil female aviator determined to chart her own course in life, at any cost: an "epic trip—through Prohibition and World War II, from Montana to London to present-day Hollywood—and you'll relish every minute" (People).

After being rescued as infants from a sinking ocean liner in 1914, Marian and Jamie Graves are raised by their dissolute uncle in Missoula, Montana. There–after encountering a pair of barnstorming pilots passing through town in beat-up biplanes–Marian commences her lifelong love affair with flight. At fourteen she drops out of school and finds an unexpected and dangerous patron in a wealthy bootlegger who provides a plane and subsidizes her lessons, an arrangement that will haunt her for the rest of her life, even as it allows her to fulfill her destiny: circumnavigating the globe by flying over the North and South Poles.

A century later, Hadley Baxter is cast to play Marian in a film that centers on Marian's disappearance in Antarctica. Vibrant, canny, disgusted with the claustrophobia of Hollywood, Hadley is eager to redefine herself after a romantic film franchise has imprisoned her in the grip of cult celebrity. Her immersion into the character of Marian unfolds, thrillingly, alongside Marian's own story, as the two women's fates–and their hunger for self-determination in vastly different geographies and times–collide. Epic and emotional, meticulously researched and gloriously told, Great Circle is a monumental work of art, and a tremendous leap forward for the prodigiously gifted Maggie Shipstead.

You Have a Friend in 10A STORIES

By Maggie Shipstead

From the Booker Prize nominee and New York Times bestselling author of Great Circle, a piercing, irresistible, "immersive" (The New York Times) first collection of short stories exquisite in their craft and audacious in their range.

A love triangle plays out over decades on a Montana dude ranch. A hurdler and a gymnast spend a single night together in the Olympic village. Mistakes and mysteries weave an intangible web around an old man's deathbed in Paris, connecting disparate destinies. On the slopes of an unfinished ski resort, a young woman searches for her vanished lover. A couple's Romanian honeymoon goes ominously awry, and, in the mesmerizing title story, a former child actress breaks with her life in a Hollywood cult.

In these and other stories, knockout after knockout, Maggie Shipstead delivers another "extraordinary" (New York Times) work of fiction and seals her reputation as a writer of "breathtaking range and skill" (Kirkus Reviews). Rich in imagination and dazzling in its shapeshifting style, You Have a Friend in 10A excavates the complexities of love, sex, and life in ways unsparing and hilarious, sharp-eyed and tender.

New & Noteworthy

They Hide Short Stories to Tell in The Dark

Thirteen tales of horror as told by critically acclaimed author, Francesca Maria

Who are we if not for the monsters that we keep?

They Hide: Short Stories to Tell in the Dark collects thirteen chilling tales that weave through the shadows, exploring the nature of fear, powerlessness, and control.

- A series of murders in a New England colony
- An untamed beast in pre-revolutionary France
- A mysterious stranger who invades 18th-century Ireland
- A traveling circus that takes more than the price of admission
- A gathering of the Dark, telling tales on the longest night of the year, and more.

Come play with vampires, werewolves, ghosts, zombies, ghouls and the devil himself. Make sure you check under the bed and don't turn out the lights.

About Francesca Maria

Francesca Maria writes dark fiction surrounded by cats near the Pacific Ocean. She is the creator of the BLACK CAT CHRONICLES comic book series and her short story collection, THEY HIDE: SHORT STORIES TO TELL IN THE DARK will be out from Brigid's Gate Press in 2023. You can find her at francescamaria.com and on Twitter @Writer_of_Weird.

Think yourself confident

15 keys to increase confidence, ignite performance, & unlock your full potential

Nathalie Plamondon-Thomas's number one Amazon Bestseller to transforming negative self-talk and thrive through change

It's never going to work. You're not good enough!" Are you tired of hearing that nagging voice inside your head? And what if you could do something about it? Do you have a dream or a project that's been on the back burner for too long? Even with all your accomplishments, do you still doubt yourself sometimes?

Statistics show that 85% of people suffer from a lack of self-confidence in at least one area of their lives. Draining negative self-talk creates procrastination, stress, anxiety, and burnout. People know what they want or need to do, and yet they do the reverse—they resist change and can't

About Nathalie Plamondon-Thomas:

2021 Canadian Presenter of the Year Nathalie Plamondon-Thomas is a Confidence Expert. She is the international No.1 Bestselling Author of seventeen books about success, communication, wellness and empowerment, including a book co-written with Jim Britt and Kevin Harrington from the TV Show SHARK TANK, and endorsed by Tony Robbins. She has proven that negative self-talk, imposter syndrome, resistance to change, past trauma, and low performance can all be addressed with increased confidence. She is the Founder and CEO of the THINK Yourself® ACADEMY, offering keynotes and trainings, leading-edge online courses, laser-focus business strategies and one-on-one transformation coaching.

Over the past 30 years, Nathalie has inspired over 100,000 audience members and empowered thousands of clients internationally. She combines over 10 years of experience in human resources, 25 years in sales and over 30 years of distinguished service in the fitness industry.

"Slowly, Slowly, Slowly," said the Sloth

STORIES OF DEMENTIA, THE CAREGIVER, AND THE HUMAN BRAIN

By Eric Carle
Illustrated by Eric Carle

Slowly, slowly, slowly . . . that's the way the sloth moves. Slowly, it eats and then, slowly, it falls asleep. "What strange kind of creature is this?" the other animals wonder. Why doesn't it run or fly or play or hunt like the rest of us? "Why are you so slow?" the howler monkey inquires. But the sloth doesn't answer any questions until the jaguar asks, "Why are you so lazy?"

Anyone who has ever felt too busy will appreciate the sloth's peaceful lifestyle and realize that it's okay to take time to enjoy life. Eric Carle' s dazzling collage illustrations introduce readers to the exotic beauty of the Amazon rain forest and the many unusual animals living there.

ABOUT THE AUTHOR

Born in the United States, Eric Carle was taken as a six-year-old child by his parents back to their native country, Germany. Later, he studied at the Akademie der Bildenden Künste (Academy of Applied Arts) in Stuttgart, and returned to New York in his early twenties as a graphic designer and artist. His many picture books are now known and loved by children around the world.

In 2002, Eric and his late wife, Barbara, opened The Eric Carle Museum of Picture Book Art, in Amherst, Massachusetts, where the works of distinguished picture book artists, nationally and internationally acclaimed, are exhibited in three spacious galleries.

Eric Carle passed away in 2021, at the age of 91.

Love Is an Ex-Country

A MEMOIR

By Randa Jarrar On Tour

Category: Nonfiction

Queer. Muslim. Arab American. A proudly Fat femme. Randa Jarrar is all of these things. In this "exuberant, defiant and introspective" memoir of a cross-country road trip, she explores how to claim joy in an unraveling and hostile America (The New York Times Book Review).

Randa Jarrar is a fearless voice of dissent who has been called "politically incorrect" (Michelle Goldberg, The New York Times). As an American raised for a time in Egypt, and finding herself captivated by the story of a celebrated Egyptian belly dancer's journey across the United States in the 1940s, she sets off from her home in California to her parents' in Connecticut.

Coloring this road trip are journeys abroad and recollections of a life lived with daring. Reclaiming her autonomy after a life of survival–domestic assault as a child, and later, as a wife; threats and doxxing after her viral tweet about Barbara Bush–Jarrar offers a bold look at domestic violence, single motherhood, and sexuality through the lens of the punished-yet-triumphant body. On the way, she schools a rest-stop racist, destroys Confederate flags in the desert, and visits the Chicago neighborhood where her immigrant parents first lived.

Hailed as "one of the finest writers of her generation" (Laila Lalami), Jarrar delivers a euphoric and critical, funny and profound memoir that will speak to anyone who has felt erased, asserting: I am here. I am joyful.

Take A Seat
ROSE GEER-ROBBINS
Author of The Writer and the Librarian
Talks

This is a beautifully written novel that will leave pure fantasy enthusiasts smitten. It includes stories within stories, carefully crafted (and magical) characters, and a wonderful plot with a touch of romance.

Author of The Writer and the Librarian, The Raven Society Book 1- Rose.L. Geer-Robbins is a reader, veteran, author, blogger, connoisseur of all things coffee, and a self-proclaimed Beat Saber expert. She is married, with three boys, two dogs, 24 snakes, and enough books to be considered a library, according to Google.

During her career of 20+ years in the U.S. Army, she had the opportunity to travel to places that had only been a tiny dot on a map. During these adventures, she discovered the power of myths, folk tales, and oral histories, which led her to pursue higher education in history and preservation.

She now writes to reconnect and rediscover stories and truths lost to the pages of history.

What kind of reader were you as a child?

I can say with certainty that I didn't have as many friends as I should have because I preferred books to playing outside. Once I figured out that you could get free pizza for reading, it was a game changer. No book was off-limits, all while eating a pepperoni personal-size pizza.

What books and authors have impacted your writing career?

A Knight in Shining Armor by Jude Deveraux that I "borrowed" from my mother. This was the first book I read that showed me you could combine history with a modern flare and romance. I don't remember how I found The Historian by Elizabeth Kostova but thank goodness I did. It inspired me to continue my education as a historian and combine it with my love of writing.

What books are you embarrassed not to have read yet?

As long as you promise not to tell anyone, I will admit that I have not read most of the classics. Moby-Dick, Frankenstein, The Grapes of Warth, Dracula, Mary Poppins, The Great Gatsby, or anything Shakespeare. But I have seen most of the movies, so there is that.

What genres do you especially enjoy reading?

Anything that revolves around history or fantasy. But just like life, my taste for books flows with the seasons. One day I might be waving a magic wand with J.K. Rowlings, and the next, I might solve a thousand-year-old mystery with Dan Brown.

Who are your fa-vorite writers? Are there any who aren't as widely known as they should be, whom you'd recommend in particular?

This is a difficult question. What if I forget an author and miss a chance to become besties with them? Some of my favorites are Alison Weir, Edward Rutherfurd, Diana Gabaldon, and Holly Black. I recently discovered Emily McIntire, who is pushing boundaries. Her retelling of classics with a whole lot of spice will make you question the norms of society.

Which writer would you want to write your life story?

Stephen Fry! Stephen Fry is the Morgan Freeman of books and history. It would be an honor to have him add his flare to my life, which has accumulated in a concerning coffee addiction, premature wrinkles, and questionable fashion sense. Call me Stephen!

Who is your favorite fictional hero or heroine?

Addie LaRue from The Invisible Life of Addie LaRue by V.E. Schwab. As a middle-aged woman, I know what it feels like to be invisible and forgettable. But Addie found a way to work around not being seen. She became memorable. Through Addie, I realized what is meaningful is not always the 'now' but 'what' legacy I will leave behind.

What book are you planning to read next?

An old friend that I have been thinking about lately- The Thirteenth Tale by Dian Setterfield. It is a remarkable example of the art of storytelling, human nature, and family and is one of my 'go-to' books.

The Modern Author Is Here!
RUSS WILLIAMS

AN EXCLUSIVE CONVERSATION

Russ Williams is the author of two self-published books, Free House and The Earth's Kidneys. He also has two active blogs, Brawd Autistico and Where the Folk. His short piece Brawd Autistico: Your Brother isn't like Other Brothers appears in Helen Bucke's Bearing Untold Stories. His first traditionally published book will be released in 2024. You can find out more on his official website, russwilliams.org.

What books are you embarrassed not to have read yet?

I kind of feel excluded from the cool club having not read any of the Harry Potters. Is it the cool club? Who knows. Same goes for Game of Thrones. I'm also ashamed to say that my grandparents got me the complete edition of The Lord of the Rings nearly two decades ago and I haven't made it past the introductory notes yet, which to be fair are pretty full-on!

You're organizing a party. Which two authors, dead or alive, do you invite?

A night with Dylan Thomas and Jack Kerouac would be a good laugh, though you can guarantee it'll be an all-nighter! At first I thought Hunter S. Thompson, but I don't think I could handle that kind of night.

Does writing energize or exhaust you?

Both, but that's only because I never do anything in proportion. If I have a free night, I tend to type away for hours at a time, emerging from the other end a bewildered mess, but done within my mental limits, writing definitely energizes me. If I ever feel anxious or down, writing almost certainly puts me in a better mood and I often feel more optimistic about life in general afterwards.

Does a big ego help or hurt writers?

I think your ego needs to be somewhere in the Goldilocks Zone to be a good writer. It's easy to be offended or put off by critics and rejections or when you see some C-list celebrity's poorly-written book sitting comfortably in the top ten. But I think the opportunity to self-publish means that many aspiring authors are too eager to get their books out there and the quality suffers as a result. They don't seek advice, or don't listen to it, at least.

On the flipside, if you didn't have any faith in yourself whatsoever and kept your writing to yourself, then you could be hiding away the next best-seller and may never know about it. You can't count on your work being discovered after you die- you need to get it out there. If you believe in yourself, show off, just don't get too ahead of yourself.

Do you try more to be original or to deliver to readers what they want?

I think the golden rule is always to write for yourself. Your voice and your passion will truly shine through if you do this. Never try to emulate. That being said, I think it's important to read other people's work so as to develop as a writer.

What was the best money you ever spent as a writer?

Without a doubt, it was the £20 or so I spent on buying the latest Writers and Artists' Yearbook. A new one comes out each year and it's essentially an A-Z of all the publishers, literary agents and so on that are out there, including information on their preferred genres and styles. This will be your literary Bible!

How did publishing your first book change your process of writing?

Ironically, my upcoming debut book it a non-fiction piece, so I'm stepping out of my comfort zone. What the process has taught me so far is not to rush so much. Get the first draft down, sure, and write that for yourself. When it comes to editing, take your time and read as though you're reading it to an audience.

The added pressure helps pick out loose ends. Also, as important as it is to have your own voice, do your best to stick to the rules. Otherwise, you run the risk of confusing individualism with poor writing.

As a writer, what would you choose as your spirit animal?

I know it's not very exciting, but I found out when writing The Earth's Kidneys that my Native American Animal Totem is a beaver. Beavers long for adventure but love the comfort of their own home- sounds about right for a writer!

A conversation with
Dana Burtin

As a young child, I disliked reading. As a teenager, I would only read for school assignments. At 19 or 20 years old, I read because I was not satisfied with the answers to my sporadic questions. Eventually, reading became an obsession to find truth.

Dana Burtin is an author from Cleveland, Ohio. Writing with the intention of increasing public knowledge and achieving common understanding, Burtin writes in a conglomerate of styles. Most notably, he writes poems, autobiographical content, historical content, and compositions that hint at a bigger picture of morality.

What's the last great book you read?

The last great book I read is entitled, Nag Hammadi.

What's your favorite book no one else has heard of?

Two of my favorite books that no one else has heard of are called, The Kybalion and None Dare Call It Conspiracy.

Are there any classic novels that you only recently read for the first time?

A classic novel that I just got around to reading is, Uncle Tom's Cabin.

Which writer would you want to write your life story?

I think I would like James Baldwin to document my life and write a book on it.

What books do you find yourself returning to again and again?

The Bible. The more I experience in life, the more I understand the allegories within.

What moves you most in a work of literature?

Taking chances. Bending the "rules". I like reading things that may be considered ahead of its time. To do this, the writer must be brave enough to take risks.

What kind of reader were you as a child?

As a young child, I disliked reading. As a teenager, I would only read for school assignments. At 19 or 20 years old, I read because I was not satisfied with the answers to my sporadic questions. Eventually, reading became an obsession to find truth.

You're organizing a party. Which two authors, dead or alive, do you invite?

I would invite James Baldwin and Maya Angelou.

Who is your favorite fictional hero?

My favorite fictional hero is Spider-Man. Spider-Man's demeanor is a character I related to most growing up.

What kind of books or writers have impacted your life?

The Kybalion impacted my life in a way that provided me with answers during a long philosophical journey of uncertainty.

CREATES REALITY

MEDUSA STONE

Medusa Stone is a novelist and poet born in Spain, winner of the Humanitarian Literary Award, international blogger, and journalist.

Through her novels, Medusa Stone explores the misuse of BDSM as an excuse for sexual abuse, with vulnerable characters in the hands of powerful men and organizations. Much of his writing explores the dark nature of humanity, shining a light on human rights violations, and enacting change one story at a time.

You're organizing a party. Which two authors, dead or alive, do you invite?

Viggo Mortensen and Charles Dickens.

Which writers — working today do you admire most?

Anne Rice, James Patterson, Carlos Ruiz Zafón, Cormac McCarthy, Paulo Coelho… Too many to mention.

Who are your favorite writers? Are there any who aren't as widely known as they should be, whom you'd recommend in particular?

Dusk Peterson, author of The Eternal

"The world thanks Author Medusa Stone for taking us up close and behind the doors of severely abused kids…The author brings awareness to the horror of the unknown. In the end, you'll want to stand-up and make a difference too!" **Author Sparkle Riley** *(Amazon reviews).*

Dungeon series, is one of my favorite authors. His writing is daring, innovating, and psychologically brilliant. I consider every book a dark, mind-bending masterpiece that should be more recognized than it currently is.

What do you read when you're working on a book? And what kind of reading do you avoid while writing?

I read books in my same genre, to assess the competition, analyze what appeals to my ideal readers are receive inspiration. Some of my most read authors are Cara Dee, Ashlyn Drewek, and Adara Wolf.

I usually avoid stressful material.

What kind of reader were you as a child?

An avid reader! My greatest inspirations were "E.T. the Extraterrestrial" by William Kotzwinkle, "Ivanhoe" by Walter Scott and "Frankenstein" by Mary Shelley. All adventurous and fantastic.

Which writer would you want to write your life story?

Carlos Ruiz Zafón, a contemporary Spanish author able to mix real scenarios with the wildest variety of characters, making each story intriguing, mysterious and exciting, while their characters are relatable and down to earth.

What books do you find yourself returning to again and again?

Books like The Purpose Driven Life by Rick Warren and The Secret by Rhonda Byrne.

What would you like to accomplish with your books?

I would like to raise awareness for all the victims of sexual abuse and sex trafficking, whilst also teaching my readers to be compassionate and not to judge, by showing them how survival can push people to their limits and force them to make the choices that few would understand.

Profits win as Women's Rights in the U.S. Violated Again!?!

Uproar over the suspect dismantling of a 170-year-old institution dedicated to women's education!

OAKLAND, CA

In current times, America is indeed broken. From over-turned abortion laws, to senseless shootings in churches and public establishments, and inflation at an all-time high leaving people and families hungry and scrimping and saving to live, no industry is safe in today's America and apparently, that also includes education, as once again profits are chosen over longevity and history!

For 170 years, Mills College has been a highly respected institution representing women's liberal arts, at the same time as California became a state. It has evolved to become a model for diversity in higher education, along with offering excellence in the liberal arts. Mills is also one of the largest urban college campuses in the country, and the parklike campus is a resource of safety and recreation in East Oakland.

But that all changed in March 2021 when Mills' president Beth Hillman suddenly announced the closure of Mills, citing "economic burdens," and characterizing its financial health as dire. In reality, and not known to the general public, Mills' endowment is currently valued at $226 M. It grew by over $39 million in the previous year alone and the college has over $73 million invested in offshore private equity and venture capital funds. Since the 2020 audit, Mills College was cash positive and had successfully paid down its debt, including raising 9.4 million in donations which was 2.6 million over its goal.

So, why the closure???? An or-

ganization has been formed called the "Save Mills College Coalition" to answer that very question and the findings were very disarming. The fact is, during Hillman's tenure, there was increasing administrative spending - until it exceeded all other budgets, even the budget for instruction - despite declaring a financial emergency. The administration carelessly overspent - by millions - on external contractors, far above rates that other colleges in close proximity pay for similar services. In addition, the trustees did not even try to refinance the debt in many years, which would save the College millions and through findings no financially responsible options to save the college were seriously pursued.

Instead, the solution was to rapidly pull together disposition of Mills College entirely – first to UC Berkeley, and two months after the closure announcement, to Northeastern University. In findings, it was determined that Board documents were leaked on social media reveal a 100% bias towards selling the college, with no consideration for leadership change or bringing in turnaround experts. The Board Negotiating Committee recommended Northeastern exclusively – not even acknowledging the offer of a large university that wanted to preserve and enhance Mills' historic mission as a women's college along with its liberal arts curriculum.

Northeastern's proposal happened to perfectly address each of the Board's selection criteria and they clearly were given preferential treatment in advance, while other universities were just expressing initial interest and had no idea what those criteria were. There was also a strong indication of conflict of interest and self-dealing in that Hillman and a few trustees will benefit from Mills College's undoing.

Over and above that that, a Temporary Restraining Order was lifted in the Alumnae organization's lawsuit against the College, the Board signed a highly incomplete merger agreement the very next day, and very shortly after, Northeastern President Aoun and Hillman released simultaneous press releases, saying Hillman would be the new president of Northeastern - Mills as well as co-lead the Institute - which means she'd also "inherit" and co-direct the $226M endowment, as the Institute would supposedly sustain Mills' mission.

The bottom line is this: There is belief that this is NOT a merger – it's a takeover by Northeastern, which is described in the merger agreement as the "surviving entity." Out-of-state Northeastern would acquire all of Mills' assets, WORTH BILLIONS, simply for paying off Mills' minimal level of debt and liabilities of approximately $30M.

So, What Can Be Done About It?

Enter Joy Nordenstrom!!

She is one of the top relationship coaches in the U.S. and is the founder of the Joy of Romance Inc and the Intelligent Love Movement. She has been featured in a substantial number of media appearances, including previously writing monthly articles for Salon Magazine. She also has a vested interest in Mills College as she attended and received her MBA and Undergraduate degrees there, and wants to help get this story to the forefront however possible!!!

Joy's belief in all of this is that something has to be done about it, that elaborate profits should not be made for the very few at the expense of an institution with the history and longevity of women's rights and diversity that Mills has. Joy believes that America is good, that the country has a chance to do something right in this instance, and all she truly wants is the opportunity to talk about it and ensure that the national public has the opportunity to hear from all sides in this very delicate situation!

Sema Özevin, Photo and Video

Not Even A Single Thing Can Stop My Passion For Writing

JANE GREEN

NY Times Bestselling Author

I tend to avoid fiction when I'm working, nervous of unintentional plagiarism. Reading memoir and biography will often inspire parts of the story I'm writing, so I tend to stick to non-fiction when I'm writing.

Jane Green is the Founder, Creative Director at Emerald Audio. She is a Podcast Show Runner & Producer at DailyMail.com and NY Times Bestselling Author, Speaker and Storyteller.

Which writers — working today do you admire most?

Anyone who keeps on writing as their main career, despite the lack of support from publishers. It has become a brutal industry, and I have found it utterly demoralising. I will always write, but after twenty one novels, writing has had to become my side hustle rather than my main gig, which I never would have expected.

· Who are your favorite writers? Are there any who aren't as widely known as they should be, whom you'd recommend in particular?

I will read anything Cathleen Schine writes, same for A.M. Homes, Jean Hanff Korelitz and Stephen Macauley. They are each wonderful writers who deal with similar themes - disparate, quirky people who unwittingly come together to form a family of choice.

· What do you read when you're working on a book? And what kind of reading do you avoid while writing?

I tend to avoid fiction when I'm working, nervous of unintentional plagiarism. Reading memoir and biography will often inspire parts of the story I'm writing, so I tend to stick to non-fiction when I'm writing.

What genres do you especially enjoy reading?

I love memoir, and literary fiction with a commercial bent.

Who is your favorite fictional hero or heroine?

Catherine in Brother of the More Famous Jack by Barbara Trapido, which remains my most favorite book of all time. Her strength and fragility, following her roller coaster journey through life brings me immeasurable pleasure, no matter how many times I read it.

What kind of reader were you as a child?

A voracious one. Like so many of us authors, I was a child who was slightly on the outside, who never felt like she fitted in. The place I found my solace and joy was within the pages of books.

Which writer would you want to write your life story?

I don't think my life story is nearly interesting enough to become a book. Which means it would require someone with a very overactive imagination and a lack of ethics.

What books do you find yourself returning to again and again?

Tales of the City by Armistead Maupin. It is like visiting old friends.

What books are you embarrassed not to have read yet?

Far too many of the classics to mention, including Ulysses and the Iliad.

What do you plan to read next?

Devil Copperhead by Barbara Kingsolver, although there is a biography of Peter Beard that is whispering my name very loudly.

/janegreenauthor

/janegreen

www.emeraldaudio.net

Only The Best Books Inside!

VANESSA GROSSETT

A Literary Agent at The Authors Care Agency

"I do want to make a point clear that not all black editors will accept manuscripts; in this industry it can be a case of who you know as well."

Vanessa Grossett is a Literary Agent at The Authors Care Agency Ltd. She represents USA Today bestselling authors such as Parker J.Cole. She is also a columnists for multi award winning magazine Keep The Faith, where she writes about the publishing industry. She also has a degree in journalism, and loves a good romance movie.

Tell us about your role as a literary agent!

A literary agent's main role is to sell their authors manuscript to publishers. Agents are their author's biggest cheerleader, and at times 'counselor.' Personally for me I like to make sure that my authors are doing okay, and if they have writers block, we talk through the manuscript together to come up with ideas, as it could be a matter of the author just needing to take a break. I tend to help promote my authors books when they are on the market. I check royalty payments, statements, and contracts. The role is very varied, and I do enjoy it.

Why did you decide to become a literary agent and what qualifications do you have?

I have a degree in journalism; I particularly loved English literature in school, and writing stories. Thankful you don't need a degree per say to be a literary agent, but a good knowledge of the industry does help, networking with editors, and publishers. When I wrote my first book, I decided that though I loved writing, it wasn't something I wanted to do full time. The agency role suits me very well, as it is a behind the scenes, type of role. I love promoting, uplifting, encouraging my authors, and reading different manuscripts.

Has the publishing industry really changed their attitude towards black authors?

On the surface with some publishers it seemed to change, and new black authors were getting a chance, especially after George Floyd. Forward a couple of years later from some the same old attitudes seem to be surfacing again.

Now I am not saying that every book by a black author must be accepted by an editor, however I have witnessed the same subconscious collective attitude with some editors; in their mindset it is difficult to sell books with primarily black characters. They may also feel like they cannot work with black authors, especially male black writers due to underlying stereotypes they may have, so they come up with reasons into why a manuscript is not accepted, could be from the writing style to not having a place in the market. Yes the author does have to make sure the manuscript is strong upon first presentation, but I know that they go through rewrites, author and editor work together on the manuscript.

Another reason is working with an agency they have not worked with before, some of them are less likely to give you a chance, and stick with who they know.

Good news is there are some editors that have moved forward and publishers like Mills and Boon have definitely become more diverse. I am not just saying that because my author writes for them, it is true, they are willing to give new black authors more of a chance, and the editors are great to work with. But make sure you follow their guidelines if you are to submit. They are some great editors, publishers out there that will believe in you and your story, it is a matter of being connected with the right one for you, building a rapport.

Other good news they're more independent imprints growing, some celebrity owned as well, to give underrepresented unpublished groups a chance for those that don't want to self publish.

I do want to make a point clear that not all black editors will accept manuscripts; in this industry it can be a case of who you know as well.

What advice would you give to anyone wanting to get into publishing industry!

Get to know the industry, network, and most importantly believe in the ability that you can do the craft well, whether it will be writing or as an agent. Never doubt your ability to be successful.

It is good to join author groups like, black writers guild to get that support, advice and knowledge. Attend writer's conferences, and meet the editor conferences.

Don't judge any editor by face value. Sometimes the editor you think is the one that will accept a manuscript ends up not being the one, but someone else.

Dream Journals:
The Dream Of Dreams
MCCOLLONOUGH CEILI

Ms. Ceili began writing when asked to tell of life on a secluded island off the coast of Ireland. Since Noria's publication in 2009 McCollonough has written several stories and poems for all ages. Her latest work is a series of dream journals designed to help children and teens learn more about the dreams they have at night. McCollonough also creates a Kid's Corner for several publications in America.

What's your favorite book no one else has heard of?

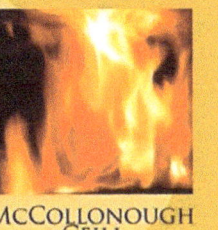

I would have to say "When the Root Children Wake Up" retold by Audrey Wood with incredible paintings by Ned Bittinger. It was the first picture book that I was able to read to myself. It is a beautiful rendition of an old German tale of a rebirth.

You're organizing a party. Which two authors, dead or alive, do you invite?

William Shakespeare and J. K. Rowling I've often wondered what the two of them were talk about if they were in the same room together.

Which writers — working today do you admire most?

All independent authors, have my biggest admiration, for are trying to build a life through a passion

Who are your favorite writers? Are there any who aren't as widely known as they should be, whom you'd recommend in particular?

I don't really have favourite authors, mostly just favourite genres which are middle grade, and historical fiction. Though, if I had to recommend an author, I would recommend Rose Bentancourt I really like all the different characters she comes up with.

What genres do you especially enjoy reading?

I absolutely love to read middle grade and historical fiction, especially those two combined into one book.

What book are you planning to read next?

Fuzzy Mud by Louis Sachar for the millionth time. I love this book.

If you could meet any writer, dead or alive, who would it be? And what would you want to know?

I don't really have favourite authors, mostly just favourite genres which are middle grade, and historical fiction. Though, if I had to recommend an author, I would recommend Rose Bentancourt I really like all the different characters she comes up with.

I would love to meet John Grisham know if he is going to write anymore, Theodore, Boone stories.

Which writer would you want to write your life story?

Steven King

POETİC AND LOVELY

Reviewed in the United States - on December 23, 2010

This is a very short book, yet it packs an emotional impact that will linger long after the book has been read. Sections are prose and sections are poetry but the whole book is filled with the kind of imagery one connects to poetry. It is as clean and refreshing as a cool bath in a mountain spring and leaves you feeling filled with questions and your own desire to see more writings from this original and delightful writer.

UNCHARTED: THE START OF THE NEW BEGINNING!

'Janet continues to draw on her rich life experiences to create engaging stories that captivate readers.

Acclaimed Author
JANET HOWLE

Janet is an accomplished author, having published the novel "Uncharted" and currently working on its sequel, which is set in the Bahamas during the 1940s when the Duke of Windsor served as Governor General amid accusations of Nazi connections.

Janet Howle is a writer and entrepreneur with a background in physical therapy. She grew up in Michigan and survived polio at a young age. After earning her BS in physical therapy from the University of Michigan, she specialized in pediatrics and later pursued graduate studies at the University of North Carolina. She spent many years as a clinician and assistant professor, writing nonfiction articles and academic papers.

Janet has been married twice and has six children, three of whom were adopted. She and her husband left the university system to start a business manufacturing mobility products for children with neuromuscular impairments, and invented a walker that continues to sell worldwide. They also enjoy vintage car rallies and have driven on back roads through Africa, South America, and North America.

Janet co-authored a novel with her husband, The Long Road to Paris, based on their around-the-world rally. She has also written a novel called Uncharted, set in the Bahamas during a period when the Colombian drug cartel controlled Norman's Cay. Janet published with Sistership Press, a small press that focuses on female authors who write both fiction and non-fiction books based on life on the water. She is currently working on a sequel to Uncharted, set in the Bahamas during the 1940s.

What's your favorite book on one else has heard of?

I am sure some people know this book, and more should. My Left Foot by Christy Brown is a long-time favorite. Mr. Brown was one of 15 children raised in a Dublin slum. Not only that, he was born with a severe form of cerebral palsy and could not walk, talk, eat, or care for himself. Born in 1932, he never went to school. The very fact he wrote two books, typing with his left foot, is nothing short of amazing and his ability to find humor while describing a tough and often lonely life is remarkable. My Left Foot was made into a movie. I still own this books along with his novel, Down All the Days.

You're organizing a party. Which two authors, dead or alive, do you invite?

Only two? I would invite Abraham Verghese and Amor Towles, both brilliant writers with extraordinary imaginations. I am constantly underlining sentences in their novels (and in the case of Verghese, his two memoirs) that I wish I could emulate.

If I could include one more, it would be Ernest Hemmingway. Not because I admire his writing so much, in truth, some of his novels, I find hard to read, but because he led such an adventurous, unconventional life, even for a writer, and certainly would add to the mix. Unfortunately, I would be so intimidated by these men, I would probably only be able to come up with something stupid like, "Well, what do you think of this weather we're having?"

Which writers-working today, do you admire most?

Certainly both Verghese and Towles as stated above, but I would also include Barbara Kingsolver, Fredrik Backman, Anthony Doerr, and Delia Owens. Kingsolver's most recent novel, Demon Copperhead is a brilliant modern day retelling of David Copperfield. I admire Backman for his smooth storytelling and charming, quirky, yet believable characters. I thoroughly enjoyed Owens' novel, Where the Crawdad's Sing but more so her honest and thoughtful memoirs describing her on-site animal research in the Kalahri Desert and the remote areas of Zambia. I have read three of Doerr's novels, all very different, but I was blown away with Cloud Cuckoo Land. I could not imagine how he was going to pull together these three time lines and he nailed it. Brilliant. (note to self: find a synonym for brilliant.)

What do you read when you're working on a book? What kind of reading do you avoid while writing?

At the stage that I am researching background for my novels, I read both fiction and non-fiction based on the factual parts of my novels. During the early stages of writing UNCHARTED, I read many books about the years the Colombian drug cartel operated in the Bahamas. When I include factual information, I want to get it right. I am currently reading books about the time the Duke of Windsor governed in the Bahamas in the 1940s as this plays a role in my WIP, the sequel to UNCHARTED.

I usually have a novel going as well. Some days I need a distraction from my writing. While I am not usually not a fan of science fiction or fantasy, I have thoroughly enjoyed Doerr's novel. Cloud Cuckoo Land, Anthony Weir's, Project Hail Mary and TJ Klune, House in the Cerulean Sea. All with fascinating characters and elegant writing. I also read popular novels to see what people are reading and buying as I always wonder if I am writing what people are looking for.

In addition to reading to escape, I read to improve my writing by analyzing how authors advance their plots and describe characters that pull the reader in. I am also currently reading Dreyer's English, which is the only grammar book that makes me laugh while improving my writing.

What kind of reader was I as a child?

A constant one. My mother was a teacher and later a librarian. She set the bar. She always made sure both my sister and I had books. Our community library was on the corner of our street and we often walked there, usually after dinner, to check out as many books as we were allowed. My sister and I collected the popular series, Little House on the Prairie, Nancy Drew, Judy Bolten among others. (I did not read Anna of Green Gables or any in that series, not sure why) A trip to the local bookstore was often a reward. We were never without stacks of books on the tables in our house.

What genres do you especially enjoy reading?

I particularly like contemporary fiction that also introduce me to bits of history I know nothing about. The Book Woman of Troublesome Creek by Kim Richardson comes to mind as does The Lost History of Stars by Dave Boling.

It's easier to say what I don't read. I don't read horror, not when I'm writing and not when I'm not. Reality in the real world is enough. (I live in the U.S. with almost daily shootings.) I am also not a fan of sci-fi or fantasy. I have read some, but not my go-to. I did thoroughly enjoy The Good Omens by Neil Gaiman and Terry Pratchett as well as those I mentioned in my answer to question 4. I will read most anything that is well-written. I am always curious about what pulls a reader in and makes a book a best-seller.

When did you start writing?

I wrote my first piece of fiction the summer I was nine or maybe ten. It was a story about a young, bored girl who, despite an otherwise happy childhood, runs away to join a circus. It wasn't a very long story since I couldn't decide if my heroine was going to be a bareback rider or aerialist, but I did know she would wear one of those sparkly, sequined leotards and tights-pink, or maybe purple. I also had no idea how to develop a plot or describe characters.

After a long pause for career and family, I didn't write or publish a novel until I was 63. I coauthored a novel, The Long Road to Paris with my husband. It was, and still is a great plot with intriguing characters. It is based on our around the world car rally. It is, I will admit, not particularly well-written and has many grammatical and spelling errors do to the fact it was hurriedly self-edited. In fact, I'm kind of embarrassed but it's out there and someday, I hope to revise it and publish it under a different title. I have learned a lot about writing since that time.

Which writer would you want to write your life story?

I am not ready to write my story. There are parts of my life that would be hurtful to family and friends close to me and I am not willing to expose those things for the sake of a juicy autobiography. If I had to choose a writer, it would be one who writes fiction that reads almost as non-fiction. Beatriz Williams or Erik Larson come to mind. I wouldn't mind a bit of embellishment.

What books are you embarrassed not to have read yet?

I have never read Wuthering Heights by Emily Bronte or Pride and Prejudice by Jane Austin (or any of this series). Often Heathcliff and Catherine or Mr. Darcy and Elizabeth are referenced in modern stories, so I am probably missing out on things, but I still can't generate the interest to follow these stilted relationships.

Are there any classic novels that you only recently read for the first time?

I'm not sure this qualifies, but it should. I recently read the epic Lonesome Dove by Larry Mc Murtry. This is not a genre that I usually read- historical American west- and I gravitate toward novels with strong female protagonists which this certainly isn't. At 900 pages, it was a bit daunting but I decided to give it a go. It is a dramatic, authentic read and I didn't want it to end. I will read another in this tetralogy.

1How would you describe your writing?

I write first to entertain but everything I have written is based on my life experiences. Fortunately, I have had many and some unconventional ones. In addition, I want my novels to introduce readers to parts of history they may not know about. My novels are set in contemporary times and in places I know well. I do change things around to move the story forward, but the settings are authentic. All my writing involves a strong female protagonist. If I had to apply a genre, it would be suspense with a romantic subplot. However, my novels would not be considered thrillers.

I admire writers such as JK Rowling who can create alternative universes but my mind doesn't work that way.

Women's Fashion In The Work Place

BY KEITH AUERBACH

Keith B. Auerbach writes for a variety of websites including Fox Hills Mall

Discussing women's fashion and attire in the work place can lead to a discussion with Human Resources, especially in some places with outdated ideas and policies. Still, there's nothing wrong with wanting to look sharp and professional, regardless of gender. Knowing what to wear when, and how to look good doing it, is a useful trick to know in any business for anyone on the job.

FORMAL FASHION

Traditional formal fashion between the genders has differed in two specific aspects: ties and skirts. In some realms, women wearing ties is expected, usually in school uniforms. In modern times, both ties for women and pants instead of skirts are generally acceptable. Places where skirts are required for women tend to veer away from proper formal attire. The basics, of course, remain the same. A suit or formal outfit, depending on the job's requirements, remain excellent options. Always remember, though, that heels are terrible and should feel terrible.

SEMI-DRESS

Semi-dress, also known as semi-formal, can be tricky to pin down because it can vary on the occasion and, unfortunately, the gender. For women, semi-dress usually means, well, a dress. In modern times suits, just as with men, are often acceptable as well. A skirted suit would work, too, depending on the job. Knowing the job's dress code is important, though in places where semi-dress is permitted it's less likely to be a safety issue. Still, it never hurts to check. The main difference between formal and semi-dress is you can reduce the number of layers and take off the suit jacket once you're at your desk.

CASUAL

Casual attire at work often depends on the job and whether or not it is Friday. For some places, it means you can wear blue jeans and a sports jersey, especially in the fall or spring. For other locations, it can mean dress slacks and either a polo or buttoned shirt. Skirts and dresses are usually acceptable as well, though, as usual, it depends on the job and the dress code. Generally, casual Fridays tend to allow more leeway than a casual business atmosphere, such as the sports team outfit during gaming season. So while some places might expect slacks or a skirt and polo as general attire, Fridays you might be allowed to wear more or less what you would on a trip to the grocery store, within reason.

Knowing what to wear at work can be tricky for both genders, but women have old-fashioned double standards to shake on top of that. Still, there's nothing wrong with looking sharp. A suit or formal day dress has a place, as do blue jeans and polo shirts. Wherever you work, be familiar with the dress code, wear comfortable shoes, and keep any jewelry to a tasteful and safe minimum. Watches are almost always acceptable, though smart watch usage might depend on company policy. Either way, make sure to know the codes so that you can look professional and, most importantly, be comfortable for the shift.

Keith B. Auerbach writes for a variety of websites including Fox Hills Mall

PHOTO: MOOSE PHOTOS

The Wonderful Benefits of Yoga

BY DR. AMAKA NWOZO

Yoga is a group of physical, mental, and spiritual practices that originated from India. There are many Yoga practices, the most common being hatha yoga and Raja yoga

It is an exercise because it improves flexibility, building strength and developing control in the body.

Countless studies show us that physical exercise is very important for the body. Exercise is physical activity that enhances physical fitness. There are a lot of benefits associated with regular exercise such as reducing the risk of diseases such as heart disease, type 2 diabetes and cancer.

Exercise also increases oxygen and blood supply to the muscles and organs of the body. It reduces bad cholesterol and increases good cholesterol. Exercise is also a great mood enhancer because it helps to reduce depression and anxiety according to research studies. Incorporating lifestyle changes like exercising can go a long way in improving health and increasing longevity.

BENEFITS OF YOGA

Weight Loss: It's great for weight loss because you burn a lot of calories when stretching and toning your body. You're losing weight while having fun. What's better than that?

Yoga improves your body by tightening, toning and strengthening it. It also makes it more flexible at the same time.

Mental Health Improvement: Yoga helps to improve mental health as studies show that regular yoga practice increases brain GABA levels, improves mood and anxiety more than some other exercises like walking. Increased relaxation is very beneficial for reducing stress.

Asthma Symptom Reduction: It has been shown to reduce symptoms of asthma in asthmatics.

Enhances Heart Health: Yoga improves heart health. It may reduce high blood pressure, improve symptoms of heart failure, enhance cardiac rehabilitation, and lower cardiovascular risk factors.

Back Pain Treatment: Yoga is also great for treating chronic low back pain. The Yoga for Healthy Lower Backs program has been found 30% more beneficial than usual care alone in a clinical trial. Pain for yoga participants decreased by a third, while the standard treatment group had only a 5% drop. Yoga participants also had a drop of 80% in the use of pain medication.

Complementary cancer treatment: Yoga is used as a complementary intervention for cancer patients to decrease depression, anxiety, insomnia, pain and fatigue.

Complementary treatment for schizophrenia: Yoga has been studied as a complementary treatment for schizophrenia. It may help alleviate symptoms of schizophrenia and improve quality of life.

Increases Cognition: Yoga has been shown to produce cognitive (executive functioning, including inhibitory control) acute benefits.

I have more information about yoga on my website, mindbodyslim.com so feel free to check it out. Yoga is amazing in making the body more flexible and toned and the benefits are enormous. Try it. You'll love it!

As a wellness specialist and health care practitioner, I love to provide people with information on how they can live their best lives. My company,mindbodyslim.com, brings you the best in fitness, active wear, recipes, skin care, kitchen essentials, and supplements for the whole mind and body. We are dedicated to helping people live their lives to the max. Sign up for wellness tips and exclusive offers at mindbodyslim.com. Come and join us! We can't wait to see you!

Skin Care Tips

Any good skincare routine should combine a cleanser followed by a toner, then a serum and lastly a moisturiser.

BY LEE ROSHAN-NAHAD

We all like to look our best. If we had the ability to choose to have smooth, beautiful and glowing skin then we would. It's a no-brainer. Choosing to have a solid skin care routine is certainly one of the ways to ensuring that this is achievable.

But what is a good skin care routine? Is there a one-size fits all?... Unfortunately no. We all have different skin types and each skin type will need it's own special, loving care. So the question then is, how do I know what is good for me?

Whether you have dry, oily, combination, sensitive or acne prone skin we will try to give a basic, easy to understand guide on how to start your journey into the sometimes overwhelming world of skin care products.

Any good skincare routine should combine a cleanser followed by a toner, then a serum and lastly a moisturiser.

The cleanser that you choose should be one that matches your individual skin requirements. For oily/combination/acne prone skin a good place to start would be a gel cleanser or something like Elizabeth's Arden Visible Difference Skin Balancing Exfoliating Cleanser for combination skin to ensure that not too much oil is added. If you have dry skin then something like a cream cleanser would be best for you. StriVectin Comforting Cream Cleanser would be ideal for this.

Next, we would recommend some sort of toner. There are three main categories for choosing a toner. First, if you have dry skin then a toner with little to no alcohol would be best. Alcohol can dry out your skin so stay away from it if you can. Lancôme Tonique Confort Hydrating Toner would be something that we would suggest for this. If you have oily skin then you may want to choose a that also exfoliates. This is because of the increased likelihood of oil becoming trapped in your pores and possibly causing breakouts. If you have combination skin then it's a bit of a judgement call but you could go for either type of cleanser but again, try to stay away from any that include alcohol, especially if it is a high concentration.

Next comes the serum. People may ask if it is necessary to use both a serum and a moisturiser... well if you want the best results then yes it is. A serum is designed to give your skin deeper reaching benefits than a moisturiser can. They penetrate down into the epidermis and provide a concentrated boost of essential nourishment to your skin. The various types of serums include, brightening serums, exfoliating serums, anti ageing serums, hydrating serums and firming serums. Depending on what you hope to achieve and what your skin needs will, obviously dictate what you choose.

And lastly, moisturisers. There are countless different moisturisers out there but for simplicity we have grouped them into 3 main categories. Humectants, Emollients and Occlusive. In a nutshell humectants are designed for people with dry skin primarily and help to seal in water to hydrate the epidermis (the top layers of skin). They do this by drawing in water from the surrounding air and by pulling water up from the dermis (the layer beneath the epidermis) to hydrate the surface skin layers. These are also great if you have oily skin but still want to moisturise as they won't add any excess oil to your skin. Emollients are great because they replicate the action of the oils naturally found in your skin. It may also help reduce the amount of insensible fluid loss (we all lose an indeterminate about of water each day, partially through the gaps between the skin cells) by filling the gaps between skin cells. Lastly in our list is the Occlusives. These are designed for extremely dry skin or for people with conditions such as eczema. They create a physical barrier in between your skin and your surroundings, sealing in moisture and protecting from further water loss. These are understandably very thick when compared to other moisturisers.

Whatever your skin care needs are we hope you find what you are looking for. Never be afraid to ask for help from experts working in beauty departments, it's what they are there for and I'm sure they will be happy to help!

Think yourself confident

15 keys to increase confidence, ignite performance, & unlock your full potential

Nathalie Plamondon-Thomas's number one Amazon Bestseller to transforming negative self-talk and thrive through change

"The way Nathalie explained how to reframe my thinking around one major obstacle will unlock potentially millions of dollars in revenue."
-Greg Schinkel; *President of Unique Training Development*

It's never going to work. You're not good enough!" Are you tired of hearing that nagging voice inside your head? And what if you could do something about it? Do you have a dream or a project that's been on the back burner for too long? Even with all your accomplishments, do you still doubt yourself sometimes?

Statistics show that 85% of people suffer from a lack of self-confidence in at least one area of their lives. Draining negative self-talk creates procrastination, stress, anxiety, and burnout. People know what they want or need to do, and yet they do the reverse—they resist change and can't adapt to the fast world we live in. That makes them feel powerless, frustrated, and insecure. In a work environment, this can lead to a demotivated and unhappy team, low overall performance and a high

employee turnover rate. With the layers of stress people are already buried under, important decisions are clouded by emotions or limiting beliefs, instead of being based on skills and experience. Bottom line: whether on a personal or professional level, most people admit to not working—or living—at their full potential.

Through Nathalie's D.N.A. System, you will discover 15 proven Keys to Confidence, real-life, simple skills and strategies to transform your inner thoughts and beliefs into a serving force that will empower you to be your best. Get ready to ignite performance and get the tools you need to THINK Yourself® CONFIDENT.

ABOUT NATHALIE PLAMONDON-THOMAS

2021 Canadian Presenter of the Year Nathalie Plamondon-Thomas is a Confidence Expert. She is the international No.1 Bestselling Author of seventeen books about success, communication, wellness and empowerment, including a book co-written with Jim Britt and Kevin Harrington from the TV Show SHARK TANK, and endorsed by Tony Robbins. She has proven that negative self-talk, imposter syndrome, resistance to change, past trauma, and low performance can all be addressed with increased confidence.

She is the Founder and CEO of the THINK Yourself® ACADEMY, offering keynotes and trainings, leading-edge online courses, laser-focus business strategies and one-on-one transformation coaching.

Over the past 30 years, Nathalie has inspired over 100,000 audience members and empowered thousands of clients internationally. She combines over 10 years of experience in human resources, 25 years in sales and over 30 years of distinguished service in the fitness industry.

Foot and Ankle Safety Tips
for the Summer Mont

From the beach to the backyard, taking care of your feet and ankles in summer is essential.

"Nothing ruins summer fun faster than a problem with your feet. However, a few smart precautions can help keep you healthy and safe," says Gretchen Lawrence, DPM, AACFAS, a board-certified foot and ankle surgeon and an associate member of the American College of Foot and Ankle Surgeons (ACFAS).

To help you understand some of the most common summer risks to feet and how to avoid them, ACFAS is sharing these insights:

• Puncture wounds: Millions of Americans go barefoot every summer, and thousands will sustain cuts and puncture wounds. To prevent injury and infection, wear shoes whenever possible and get vaccinated against tetanus. If you do get a puncture wound, see a foot and ankle surgeon within 24 hours and don't swim until it's healed. Bacteria in oceans and lakes can cause infection.

• Pool problems: Always wear flip flops or other footwear in locker rooms and on pool decks to prevent contact with bacteria and viruses that can cause

Summer sports can lead to arch pain, heel pain, ankle sprains and other injuries. Proper footwear with heel cushioning and arch support is essential, particularly on uneven surfaces, such as sandy beaches or hiking trails.

athlete's foot, plantar warts and other problems.

• Sun damage and skin cancer: Don't overlook your feet during your sun protection routine. Feet get sunburned too, and melanoma on the foot or ankle is more likely to be misdiagnosed than on any other part of the body. A study published in "The Journal of Foot & Ankle Surgery" reported the overall survival rate for melanoma of the foot or ankle is just 52%, in sharp contrast to the 85% survival rate for melanomas on other areas of the body. Apply sunscreen to the tops and bottoms of feet and limit sun exposure. Dr. Lawrence notes, "If you spot abnormal moles or pigmented skin, including under toenails, visit a foot and ankle surgeon. Early detection and treatment could save your life."

• Pains and sprains: Summer sports can lead to arch pain, heel pain, ankle sprains and other injuries. Proper footwear with heel

cushioning and arch support is essential, particularly on uneven surfaces, such as sandy beaches or hiking trails. If injury occurs, use the RICE approach: rest, ice, compression and elevation to ease pain and swelling. Any injury that doesn't resolve within a few days should be examined by a foot and ankle surgeon.

• Mower risks: Some 25,000 Americans sustain injuries from power mowers annually, according to the U.S. Consumer Products Safety Commission. Many of these injuries are preventable. Always cut the grass in protective shoes or work boots and keep children away during this chore. Never mow a wet lawn or pull the mower backward, and always mow across slopes, not up or down them.

• Travel concerns: Sitting for long stretches can increase the risk of dangerous blood clots. "Whether road tripping or flying, regularly stretch your legs and

pump your feet to circulate blood. Wearing compression socks for longer travel is also a good idea," says Dr. Lawrence.

• Diabetes complications: If you have diabetes, prolonged hot and humid weather can lead to numerous foot woes. Any type of skin break has the potential to get infected if it isn't noticed right away, and exposure can cause dry, cracking skin. Inspect your feet daily and wear closed shoes whenever possible. Swelling is another hot-weather risk, potentially making shoes fit tighter which can cause blisters. Compression stockings may not sound appealing in hot temperatures, but they can reduce swelling and help prevent poor circulation. Finally, never go barefoot in summer. Impaired nerve sensation can make it hard to detect just how hot surfaces are. Just a few minutes walking barefoot on pavement to grab the newspaper can cause third-degree burns.

For more information and to find a foot and ankle surgeon near you, visit FootHealthFacts. org, the patient education website for the American College of Foot and Ankle Surgeons.

(STATEPOINT)

Wear Contacts? Here are 5 Tips to Elevate Your Routine

If you're one of the 45 million Americans who wear contact lenses, you know what a great choice they can be, whether you play sports, want to avoid the nuisance of foggy glasses or simply find yourself feeling more confident in them. However, it may be time to give your contact lens care routine a makeover, particularly if your lenses feel dry or uncomfortable.

Unfortunately, one in five contact lens wearers find lenses to be less comfortable by the end of the day. Consider the following tips for all-day comfort:

1. Practice healthy tech habits: Long hours on screens can be a contributing factor to eye discomfort, mainly because of less blinking; however, making a few adjustments can help. The experts at Bausch + Lomb recommend following the 20-20-20 rule. For every 20 minutes of screen time, take a 20 second break to look at something 20 feet away. If you work with computers all day, you should also remember to blink regularly. It can be surprisingly easy to forget to blink when you're focused on the next deadline! Finally, adjust the brightness and text size on your devices to reduce eye strain and optimize comfort.

2. Insert and remove contacts with care: The order of steps you follow as you insert and remove your contacts matters. In the morning or as you're getting ready to go out, insert contact lenses with clean hands before applying makeup. Before bed, wash your hands, remove your contacts and clean your lenses before going to sleep. One-third of contact lens wearers have fallen asleep in their lenses, but doing so increases the risk of infection.

3. Follow lens care directions: According to the Centers for Disease Control and Prevention, 40-90% of contact lens wearers do not properly follow their contact lenses' care instructions. It is recommended to follow the complete recommended lens rubbing and rinsing times in the product labeling to adequately disinfect your lenses and reduce the risk of contact lens contamination. Reduced rubbing or rinsing time may not adequately clean your lenses. And never "top off" or reuse solution. Fill the lens case with fresh solution every time you store your lenses – don't cut corners!

4. Clean and moisturize: One in three contact lens wearers experiences dry lenses, and one in five find lenses to be less comfortable by the end of the day. Show your eyes some love by using a contact lens solution recommended by board-certified optometrists, one that is uniquely-formulated for dry, uncomfortable contact lenses. Biotrue Hydration Plus Multi-Purpose Solution not only offers exceptional cleaning and disinfection and dissolves protein build-up, it's also formulated with your eyes' biology in mind to promote all-day comfort. It contains naturally-inspired ingredients found in tears such as hyaluronan, a moisturizer, and potassium, an electrolyte. It keeps more moisture on your contacts (for 12 hours compared to original Biotrue Multi-Purpose Solution, based on a laboratory study) as well as provides up to 20 hours of moisture (based on a laboratory study). For more information and complete use instructions, visit https://www.biotrue.com.

5. Recycle: While not directly related to the comfort of your eyes, you can sport your contacts with more ease knowing you're doing so with the environment in mind. You're likely already recycling contact solution bottles and eye care product cartons through curbside recycling. Now, thanks to a collaboration between Bausch + Lomb and TerraCycle, there's a way to properly recycle the smaller plastic components within these products. Pop off the caps of your solution and eye drop bottles and place them in any shipping box, along with old lens cases, empty eye drop bottles and single dose eye drop vials. When the box is full, print the prepaid label and mail it to TerraCycle. These components are combined with other recycled materials and turned into new products. To learn more, visit terracycle.com/biotrue.

Stop chalking up dry, uncomfortable lenses to being a regular part of wearing contacts. With a few tweaks to your routine, you can experience comfort throughout the day. Biotrue is a trademark of Bausch + Lomb Incorporated or its affiliates. ABT.0011. USA.23 (STATEPOINT)

Available both print and electronic all over the globe.
The Reader's Hosue reaches more then 40.000
retailers (including Amazon, Barnes & Noble
Waterstones, Blackwells, and local independent
bookstores in the United States.)

Visit thereadershouse.co.uk for more

The Reader's House

Save up to 50% when you
order 10 or more from the
same issue

Milton Keynes UK
Ingram Content Group UK Ltd.
UKHW050652140823
426830UK00001B/2